Trumpet Partitas
by William Bay

This is a collection of 17 unaccompanied trumpet solos. All are lively in nature and will serve as good technical studies. They are fun to play and are intentionally evocative of the baroque trumpet style. I really enjoy these pieces and hope you find them melodically and technically satisfying.

William Bay

© 2016 by William Bay. All Rights Reserved. BMI.
Sales Agent: Mel Bay Publications, Inc.
www.melbay.com

Partita #1
G minor

Lightly ♩. = 82

William Bay

Partita #5
A minor

William Bay

Allegro ♩ = 106

Partita #7
E minor

William Bay

Moderato ♩= 88

14

Partita #9
A Major

Allegro ♩=98

William Bay

Partita #10
G minor

William Bay

Partita #12
E minor

William Bay

Moderato ♩ = 112

Partita #13
E minor

William Bay

Allegro ♩ = 90

Partita #14
D minor

William Bay

Partita #15
C Major

Allegro ♩=98

William Bay

Partita #16
D minor

William Bay

Allegro ♩= 94

Partita #17
F minor

William Bay

Allegro ♩= 96

Other Trumpet Books by William Bay

Hymns for Unaccompanied Trumpet
Trumpet Ballads
Trumpet Tone Poems
Trumpet Chants
Hymns and Descants for Trumpet
Trumpet Praise
7 Festive Trumpet Solos
Complete Jazz Trumpet Book
Trumpet Handbook

Available from Mel Bay Publications Inc.
www.melbay.com

www.ingramcontent.com/pod-product-compliance
Lightning Source LLC
LaVergne TN
LVHW061257060426
835507LV00020B/2339